How to Start a Jewelry Business
The Ultimate Guide to Making and Selling Jewelry

I0086152

By Quinn Chapman

How to Start a Jewelry Business

THE ULTIMATE GUIDE TO MAKING AND SELLING JEWELRY

by Quinn Chapman

Published by TLM Publishing House

5905 Atlanta Highway, Alpharetta GA.
https://www.ttpublishinghouse.com
Copyright © 2023 TLM Publishing House

Legal Disclaimer: We utilized ChatGPT for help with research. We are making no claims, whether medical, financial, or otherwise.

Table of Contents

Introduction

Welcome to "The Ultimate Guide to Making and Selling Jewelry." In the glittering world of accessories, jewelry has always held a special place, embodying a blend of artistry, beauty, and personal expression. The allure of crafting and sharing your own jewelry creations is undeniable, as it offers not only a creative outlet but also the potential for a thriving business. This book is your key to unlocking the secrets of the jewelry-making trade, whether you're an aspiring artisan looking to turn your passion into profit or a seasoned crafter wanting to take your jewelry business to new heights.

The Essence of Jewelry

Jewelry isn't just about adorning oneself with precious metals and gemstones; it's a form of self-expression that resonates with emotions, relationships, and individual style. Each piece of jewelry tells a story, be it a delicate necklace that represents a cherished memory, a bold statement ring that exudes confidence, or an elegant bracelet that encapsulates one's personality.

The Allure of Crafting

The undeniable allure of crafting your jewelry is multifaceted. It provides a creative outlet that allows you to breathe life into your artistic visions. Whether you're drawn to the intricacies of handcrafted jewelry or the allure of designing unique pieces, this book is your guide to transforming your ideas into tangible works of art.

From Creativity to Prosperity

However, the journey of jewelry-making isn't confined to personal gratification alone. It opens the door to an exciting world of business opportunities. Whether you're a novice artisan seeking to turn your passion into a profit-generating venture or a seasoned crafter aspiring to elevate your jewelry business to new heights, this book is your compass in the jewelry-making trade.

Unveiling the Secrets

Within the pages of this comprehensive guide, you will unlock the well-guarded secrets of the jewelry-making trade. From mastering fundamental techniques to understanding the nuances of marketing and sales, this book equips you with the knowledge, skills, and strategies needed to succeed in the ever-evolving world of jewelry.

Why Jewelry Making and Selling?

Jewelry is more than just ornamental adornments; it's a reflection of our identity, a symbol of our emotions, and a means to convey our personal style. The art of jewelry-making allows individuals to tap into their creativity, transforming raw materials into wearable works of art that can inspire and enchant. But beyond artistic fulfillment, the world of jewelry holds endless opportunities for those looking to build a successful business. Here are a few compelling reasons why jewelry making and selling can be an exciting and rewarding venture:

Express Your Creativity
Jewelry-making is a craft that welcomes your artistic expression. Whether you're designing dainty necklaces, bold statement pieces, or elegant rings, you have the creative freedom to craft pieces that resonate with your unique style and personality.

Personalized Gifts
Creating custom jewelry allows you to offer heartfelt gifts to your loved ones. Craft pieces that celebrate special occasions like birthdays, anniversaries, and holidays, turning your creations into cherished tokens of love and appreciation.

Income Potential
For those with an entrepreneurial spirit, jewelry-making can be a lucrative endeavor. In today's world, there is a growing demand for unique, handcrafted jewelry,

opening the doors to a thriving business that you can operate from the comfort of your home or a dedicated studio.

Eco-Friendly and Sustainable

With the rise of sustainability and ethical consumerism, handcrafted jewelry made from eco-friendly materials has gained popularity. By adopting responsible practices, you can contribute to a greener world and appeal to environmentally conscious customers.

Who This Book Is For

"*The Ultimate Guide to Making and Selling Jewelry*" is designed for a diverse audience, each with their own unique journey into the world of jewelry. Whether you're a complete novice or an experienced jewelry maker, this book has something to offer:

Beginners: If you're new to jewelry making, this book will provide you with step-by-step instructions, tips, and essential knowledge to help you get started on your creative journey. We'll walk you through the basics and guide you towards crafting your first piece.

Intermediate Crafters: For those who have already dabbled in jewelry making, this book will help you refine your skills, introduce new techniques, and assist you in taking your craft to the next level. You'll discover how to create more intricate designs and explore various styles.

Aspiring Entrepreneurs: If you're interested in turning your passion into profit, we'll share valuable insights on how to establish and grow a successful jewelry business. You'll learn about marketing, branding, online sales, and other crucial aspects of entrepreneurship in the jewelry industry.

Experienced Artisans: Even if you have years of experience, this book will serve as a comprehensive resource to enhance your knowledge, discover the latest trends, and explore advanced techniques. Whether you're seeking inspiration or practical advice, you'll find valuable information within these pages.

Embark on Your Journey

"The Ultimate Guide to Making and Selling Jewelry" is your faithful companion on the journey of jewelry-making and sales. Whether you seek to craft dazzling pieces, create a successful business, or both, this guide is the key to unlocking the limitless potential of the jewelry world. Are you ready to dive headfirst into the enchanting world of jewelry? Let's begin.

Chapter 1

Getting Started in Jewelry Making

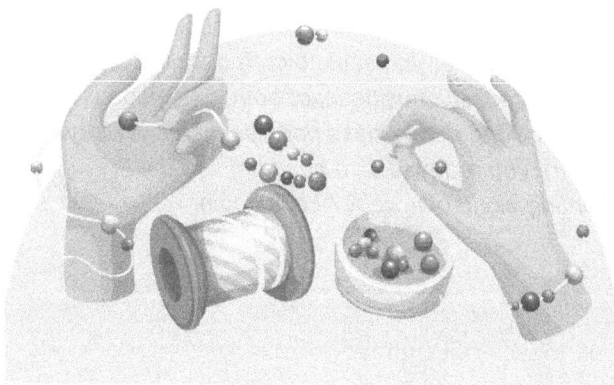

Chapter 1: Getting Started in Jewelry Making

Jewelry making is a rewarding and creative craft that offers endless possibilities for self-expression and entrepreneurship. In this chapter, we'll guide you through the foundational aspects of getting started in jewelry making, ensuring that you have a strong knowledge base before you begin crafting your own beautiful pieces.

Understanding the Basics of Jewelry Making

To embark on your journey into the world of jewelry making, it's essential to grasp the foundational principles that underpin this craft. This understanding will serve as the solid ground upon which you'll build your creative endeavors.

Anatomy of Jewelry

Before you can create your own unique jewelry pieces, it's essential to have a solid understanding of the fundamental components that make up a piece of jewelry. The anatomy of jewelry is like the alphabet of the craft; mastering these basic elements is the key to constructing beautiful, harmonious, and structurally sound pieces.

Main Elements

- *Gemstones:* Gemstones are the stars of the show in many pieces of jewelry. They come in a wide variety of colors, shapes, and sizes, and they add a touch of elegance and value to your creations. Understanding the types of gemstones, their properties, and how to handle them is crucial. From the fiery brilliance of diamonds to the vivid hues of sapphires and emeralds, you'll discover how to choose, set, and care for these precious stones.

- *Beads:* Beads are versatile components in jewelry making, available in countless materials and styles. They can be strung together to create stunning necklaces or bracelets, and their unique shapes and colors can add character and flair to your designs. Learn about the different types of beads, how to incorporate them into your creations, and the techniques for beadwork.

- *Metals:* Metals are the foundation of many jewelry pieces. Gold, silver, platinum, and copper are among the most common metals used in jewelry making. You'll explore the characteristics of these metals, their properties, and how to work with them. Whether you're aiming for a luxurious gold pendant or a sleek silver ring, understanding the intricacies of metalworking is essential.

Settings and Findings

- *Settings:* Settings are the components that secure gemstones in place within a piece of jewelry. These can vary from prong settings that hold a gemstone in place with metal claws to bezel settings that encircle the gemstone with a metal rim. Different settings have distinct advantages and appearances, and you'll discover how to select and use them effectively.

- *Findings:* Findings are the small elements that help you connect and finish your jewelry pieces. This includes clasps for necklaces and bracelets, earring hooks, jump rings, and more. Learning how to choose the right findings for your designs and how to attach them securely is crucial for creating functional and durable jewelry.

Understanding the anatomy of jewelry is not just about recognizing its components; it's about appreciating how each element contributes to the overall aesthetics, structure, and functionality of a piece. Mastery of these elements will enable you to craft jewelry that is not only visually pleasing but also sturdy and long-lasting. As you delve deeper into jewelry making, this foundational knowledge will be the cornerstone of your creative endeavors.

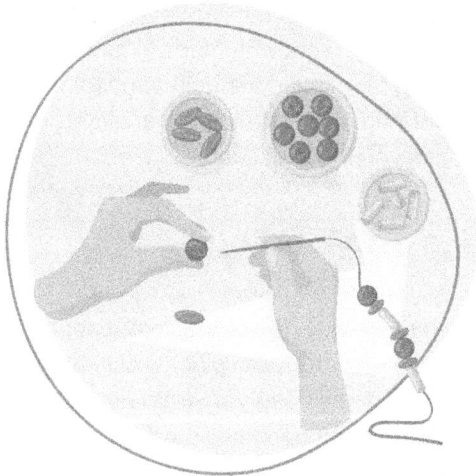

Styles and Techniques

Jewelry making encompasses a wide range of styles and techniques, each with its unique characteristics and appeal. Exploring these diverse approaches will empower you to find the methods that resonate most with your creative vision. Here, we'll dive deeper into the world of styles and techniques, providing you with a more comprehensive understanding.

Styles

- Wire Wrapping: Wire wrapping is a versatile technique that involves shaping and securing wires around gemstones, beads, or other components. It allows for intricate and organic designs, making it a popular choice for crafting unique pendants, earrings, and rings.

- Beadwork: Beadwork is a precise art that involves stringing and weaving beads into intricate patterns. It offers a vast array of possibilities in terms of colors, shapes, and designs. From simple and elegant to complex and ornate, beadwork allows you to create pieces that reflect your personal style.

- Metalworking: Metalworking includes various processes such as soldering, forging, and casting to shape and manipulate metals like gold, silver, and copper. This technique is ideal for those who appreciate the craft of working with precious metals and creating bespoke pieces.

11

- Polymer Clay: Polymer clay is a versatile material that can be molded, sculpted, and baked to create colorful and unique jewelry. It's a medium that encourages artistic expression and is especially popular for crafting statement pieces and artisan jewelry.

Techniques

- Wire Work: Wire work involves bending, shaping, and securing wire to create various components of jewelry, such as clasps, links, and decorative elements. Understanding wire gauges, types, and techniques is essential for mastering this versatile method.

- Beading Techniques: Beadwork encompasses a wide range of techniques, including stringing, peyote stitch, brick stitch, and more. Each technique offers different opportunities for creating intricate patterns and textures.

- Soldering: Soldering is a metalworking technique that involves joining pieces of metal using a solder alloy. It's an essential skill for creating metal jewelry and ensures secure connections in your designs.

- Enameling: Enameling is the process of fusing glass to metal. This technique allows for a wide range of colors and effects, adding a vibrant and lasting dimension to your pieces.

- Clay Sculpting: Polymer clay sculpting is a hands-on approach to crafting intricate and detailed components. It's an ideal technique for creating custom beads, pendants, and embellishments.

Each style and technique offers a unique set of possibilities and challenges, allowing you to express your creativity in diverse ways. As you delve deeper into the world of jewelry making, consider exploring multiple styles and techniques to expand your repertoire and craft a wide range of jewelry pieces, from delicate and intricate to bold and statement-making. This comprehensive understanding of styles and techniques will form the bedrock of your creative journey in jewelry making.

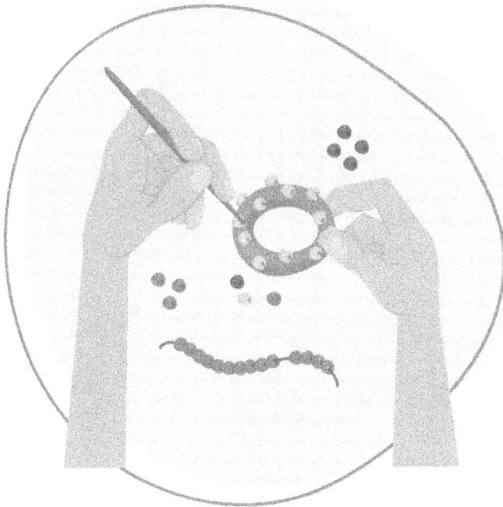

Design Principles

Design principles are the essential guidelines that transform a collection of materials into aesthetically pleasing and harmonious jewelry pieces. Grasping these principles is crucial for creating jewelry that not only looks beautiful but also resonates with your unique vision. Here, we'll delve deeper into the world of design principles, providing you with a more comprehensive understanding.

Balance

- Symmetry: Achieving symmetry in a jewelry piece means that one side mirrors the other, creating a sense of equilibrium. Symmetrical designs are often associated with formality and elegance, making them suitable for classic and timeless pieces.

- Asymmetry: Asymmetry involves creating visual balance through uneven distribution. It allows for more creative and dynamic designs, making it ideal for contemporary and artisan jewelry that seeks to break traditional boundaries.

Color Theory

- Color Harmony: Understanding color harmony is key to creating jewelry with a pleasing color palette. Different color schemes, such as complementary (opposite colors on the color wheel) or analogous (colors adjacent to each other on the wheel), can be used to evoke specific emotions and moods in your designs.

- Contrast: Contrast in color involves using color opposites or emphasizing differences to create visual interest. Bold contrasts can make your jewelry pieces stand out, while subtle contrasts can add depth and dimension.

Proportion and Scale

- Proportion: Proportion refers to the relationship between different elements in your jewelry piece. Understanding how elements like gemstones, beads, and metal components interact in size and shape is crucial for achieving a balanced and visually appealing design.

- Scale: Scale deals with the overall size of a jewelry piece. It's important to consider scale in relation to the wearer's body and personal style. Smaller pieces may be suitable for delicate and everyday wear, while larger pieces can make a statement or serve as statement jewelry.

Unity and Variety

- Unity: Unity in design ensures that all elements in a piece work together to create a cohesive and harmonious whole. Repeating patterns, themes, or materials can enhance unity and provide a sense of completeness in your jewelry.

16

- Variety: Variety introduces diversity and interest into your design. While unity brings everything together, variety allows for unique and eye-catching details that can make your jewelry pieces truly exceptional.

Understanding and applying these design principles will not only elevate the visual appeal of your jewelry but also infuse your creations with meaning and intention. Whether you aim to craft classic and elegant pieces that exude timeless beauty or contemporary and artistic jewelry that challenges conventions, these principles serve as your guiding light in the creative process. As you gain a deeper appreciation for design, your jewelry pieces will become not just adornments but expressions of your unique artistic vision.

Essential Tools and Materials

To bring your jewelry designs to life, you need to familiarize yourself with the essential tools and materials that will enable you to create stunning, one-of-a-kind pieces. In this section, we'll explore these critical components in more detail, providing a comprehensive understanding of what you'll need to start your journey.

Essential Tools

Pliers

1. Round-Nose Pliers: These pliers have round, tapering jaws and are ideal for creating loops, bends, and coils in wire.
2. Chain-Nose Pliers: These pliers have flat, pointed jaws and are versatile for gripping, bending, and manipulating wires and components.
3. Flat-Nose Pliers: Flat-nose pliers have flat, rectangular jaws and are useful for holding, bending, and straightening wire or metal components.
4. Crimping Pliers: Crimping pliers are specialized tools used to secure crimp beads or tubes to fasten components in beading projects.

Cutters

1. Wire Cutters: Wire cutters are designed to cut various gauges of wire cleanly and efficiently.
2. Flush Cutters: Flush cutters have flat blades that provide a flush cut on wire ends, ensuring a neat finish.

Hammers

1. Chasing Hammer: A chasing hammer is used for texturing and shaping metal.
2. Rawhide Mallet: A rawhide mallet is a non-marring hammer used to shape metal without leaving marks.

Mandrels

1. Ring Mandrel: A ring mandrel is a tapered tool used for shaping and sizing rings.
2. Bracelet Mandrel: A bracelet mandrel is a cylindrical tool for shaping and sizing bracelets and bangles.

Files

1. Needle Files: Needle files are small, precision files used for shaping and smoothing metal and other materials.

Sawframe and Blades

1. A sawframe and saw blades are essential for cutting metal sheets and wires with precision.

Measuring Tools

1. Measuring tools such as rulers, calipers, and gauges are crucial for ensuring accurate and consistent sizing in your jewelry.

Materials

Metals

1. Gold: Gold is a timeless and precious metal used in jewelry making, available in various karats for different levels of purity.
2. Silver: Silver is a popular and versatile metal known for its lustrous appearance.
3. Copper: Copper is valued for its warm, reddish hue and is often used for wirework and decorative elements in jewelry.

Gemstones

1. Gemstones come in a wide variety of types, colors, and qualities, from diamonds to sapphires, emeralds, and more.

Beads

1. Beads are available in various materials, including glass, crystal, wood, and more, and can add texture and color to your designs.

21

Wires and Cords

1. Various types of wire, such as beading wire and artistic wire, as well as cords like leather or silk, are used for stringing and designing jewelry.

Findings

1. Findings include clasps, jump rings, ear wires, and other components that help you assemble and finish your jewelry pieces.

Understanding the properties and uses of these tools and materials will empower you to make informed choices based on your project requirements and personal preferences. Whether you're aiming for elegant gold jewelry, intricate wire-wrapped designs, or vibrant beaded creations, this comprehensive knowledge will be the cornerstone of your creative endeavors.

Basic tools

Basic tools are the backbone of any jewelry-making endeavor. These tools allow you to manipulate, shape, and assemble materials effectively, ensuring that your jewelry pieces come to life with precision and skill. In this section, we'll explore the essential basic tools in more detail, providing a comprehensive understanding of their purposes and usage.

Pliers

Round-Nose Pliers

- Purpose: Round-nose pliers have rounded, tapering jaws that are ideal for creating loops, bends, and coils in wire. They are essential for making loops for earrings, pendants, and other components.
- Usage: Use round-nose pliers to form simple loops and wrapped loops, as well as to shape wire and create curved elements in your designs.

Chain-Nose Pliers:

- Purpose: Chain-nose pliers have flat, pointed jaws and are versatile for gripping, bending, and manipulating wires and components. They are essential for various tasks like opening and closing jump rings, holding small components, and making angular bends.
- Usage: Chain-nose pliers are used for tasks that require precision and control, such as making sharp bends, gripping small components, and securely closing connections.

Flat-Nose Pliers:

- Purpose: Flat-nose pliers have flat, rectangular jaws and are useful for holding, bending, and straightening wire or metal components. They provide a flat surface for gripping, making them suitable for tasks that require a firm grip without leaving impressions on the material.
- Usage: Flat-nose pliers are often used for making sharp bends, straightening wire, and holding components in place while working on your jewelry pieces.

Crimping Pliers:

- Purpose: Crimping pliers are specialized tools used to secure crimp beads or tubes to fasten components in beading projects. They create a secure and neat finish for beaded jewelry.
- Usage: Crimping pliers are essential for stringing and finishing beaded designs, ensuring that components are securely held together and that the finishing touches are polished and professional.

Cutters

Wire Cutters

- Purpose: Wire cutters are designed to cut various gauges of wire cleanly and efficiently. They are essential for creating precise and clean cuts in wire, allowing you to work with materials of different thicknesses.
- Usage: Wire cutters are used to cut wire to the desired lengths, making them indispensable for various wirework and beading projects.

Flush Cutters:

- Purpose: Flush cutters have flat blades that provide a flush cut on wire ends, ensuring a neat finish. They are particularly useful for projects where the cut wire ends should not protrude or leave sharp edges.
- Usage: Flush cutters are ideal for creating a smooth and even cut on wire, preventing any sharp or jagged edges that can be uncomfortable when worn.

These basic tools are the foundation of your jewelry-making toolkit, and mastering their usage is essential for creating well-crafted and professional-quality jewelry pieces. Whether you're bending wire, securing components, or achieving precise cuts, these tools will be your trusted companions in your creative journey.

Materials

Materials are the building blocks of your jewelry creations. Whether you're working with metals, gemstones, beads, wires, or cords, understanding the properties and characteristics of these materials is crucial for designing and crafting jewelry that's not only aesthetically pleasing but also durable and well-suited to its intended purpose. In this section, we'll explore the essential materials used in jewelry making, providing a comprehensive understanding of their unique features.

Metals

Gold:

- Properties: Gold is a timeless and precious metal known for its luster, malleability, and resistance to tarnish and corrosion. It comes in various karats, with 24k being the purest.
- Usage: Gold is often used for crafting elegant and high-value jewelry pieces, including rings, necklaces, bracelets, and earrings.

Silver:

- Properties: Silver is a popular and versatile metal cherished for its brilliant white shine. It's malleable and can be easily manipulated into intricate designs.
- Usage: Silver is commonly used in a wide range of jewelry pieces, from classic and understated designs to bold and contemporary creations.

Copper:

- Properties: Copper has a warm, reddish hue and is appreciated for its conductivity and corrosion resistance. It's an excellent choice for wirework and decorative elements in jewelry.

- Usage: Copper is often used for wire jewelry, textured components, and as a base for enameling and patination techniques.

Gemstones

Diamonds:

- Properties: Diamonds are renowned for their exceptional brilliance, hardness, and clarity. They are prized for their exceptional beauty and rarity.
- Usage: Diamonds are often featured as centerpieces in engagement rings and as accents in various jewelry designs.

Sapphires:

- Properties: Sapphires come in a range of colors, with the blue sapphire being the most well-known. They are durable and have excellent clarity and brilliance.
- Usage: Sapphires are used to add color and elegance to rings, pendants, and earrings.

Emeralds:

- Properties: Emeralds are prized for their vivid green color and natural inclusions. They are softer than diamonds and sapphires, making them suitable for certain jewelry designs.
- Usage: Emeralds are often used in jewelry pieces that emphasize their captivating green color, such as necklaces and earrings.

Beads

Glass Beads:

- Properties: Glass beads come in various colors, shapes, and sizes. They can be transparent, opaque, or frosted, offering endless creative possibilities.
- Usage: Glass beads are commonly used in beaded jewelry, adding texture and color to necklaces, bracelets, and earrings.

Crystal Beads:

- Properties: Crystal beads are known for their exceptional sparkle and clarity. They come in a variety of shapes, including bicones and rondelles.
- Usage: Crystal beads are often used to create glamorous and

eye-catching jewelry pieces for special occasions.

Wires and Cords

Beading Wire:

- Properties: Beading wire is a flexible and sturdy wire designed for stringing beads. It's typically made of stainless steel and coated with nylon for durability.
- Usage: Beading wire is essential for creating strung jewelry, such as necklaces and bracelets.

Leather Cord:

- Properties: Leather cord is durable, flexible, and available in various colors and thicknesses. It's often used for creating rustic and bohemian-style jewelry.
- Usage: Leather cord is popular for making necklaces, bracelets, and anklets, especially in designs with natural or tribal themes.

Understanding the properties, characteristics, and potential applications of these materials is fundamental to making informed choices based on your project requirements and design preferences. Whether you're crafting elegant gold jewelry, intricate beaded designs, or rustic leather pieces, this comprehensive knowledge of materials will be your foundation for creating jewelry that's both aesthetically pleasing and built to last.

Sourcing Materials

Sourcing materials is a crucial aspect of jewelry making, as the quality and availability of your materials can significantly impact the outcome of your creations. In this section, we'll delve into the essential considerations for sourcing materials, helping you make informed decisions about where and how to acquire the components for your jewelry projects.

Local Suppliers

Advantages: Local suppliers, such as jewelry supply stores, craft shops, and art supply stores, offer the advantage of immediate access to materials. You can see and feel the materials in person and get expert advice from knowledgeable staff.

Considerations: Prices at local suppliers may vary, and the selection of materials might be limited compared to online options. It's essential to explore multiple local sources to find the best options for your needs.

Online Retailers

Advantages: Online retailers provide a vast selection of jewelry-making materials, often at competitive prices. You can shop from the comfort of your home, access a wider range of options, and compare prices easily.

Considerations: When shopping online, it's important to read product descriptions, reviews, and return policies carefully. Additionally, consider shipping costs and delivery times when planning your projects.

Wholesale Suppliers

Advantages: Wholesale suppliers offer bulk quantities of materials at discounted prices. This can be advantageous if you're planning to create jewelry for sale or have ongoing projects.

Considerations: Wholesale purchasing often comes with minimum order requirements, so assess your needs before buying in bulk. Additionally, ensure that the quality of materials meets your standards.

Artisan Markets and Trade Shows

Advantages: Artisan markets and trade shows provide opportunities to source unique and handcrafted materials from independent artisans and suppliers. You can discover one-of-a-kind components and establish personal connections.

Considerations: These events may not be as readily available as local or online options, and timing may be limited. It's a good idea to plan ahead and attend these markets or shows when they occur in your area.

Recycling and Upcycling:

Advantages: Recycling and upcycling materials can be a sustainable and cost-effective approach. You can repurpose old jewelry, vintage items, or found objects to create eco-friendly and unique pieces.
Considerations: Carefully evaluate the condition and suitability of recycled materials. Some items may require cleaning, repair, or modification before use in your designs.

Community and Art Supply Swaps

Advantages: Participating in community or art supply swaps can be a fun and economical way to acquire new materials and share your excess supplies with others.
Considerations: The availability and frequency of such swaps may vary by location, so look for local groups or events that facilitate material exchanges.

Ethical and Sustainable Sourcing

Advantages: Ethical and sustainable sourcing aligns with eco-friendly and socially responsible principles. It can appeal to environmentally conscious customers and enhance the ethical value of your creations.
Considerations: Ensure that the materials you source meet ethical and sustainable standards, such as fair trade or responsibly mined gemstones.

Testing and Quality Assurance

Regardless of your sourcing method, it's essential to test and evaluate the quality of materials, especially for precious metals and gemstones. Familiarize yourself with methods to assess authenticity and quality, such as checking hallmarks and conducting gemstone tests when applicable.

Effective material sourcing is a fundamental aspect of jewelry making that can influence the quality, uniqueness, and sustainability of your creations. By considering these various sourcing options and factors, you can make informed decisions that align with your project goals and personal values. Whether you're seeking convenience, cost-effectiveness, sustainability, or uniqueness, the right sourcing approach can make your jewelry-making journey even more fulfilling.

Safety Precautions in Jewelry Making

Safety is paramount in any creative endeavor, and jewelry making is no exception. It's essential to take appropriate safety precautions to protect yourself and ensure a safe and enjoyable crafting experience. In this section, we'll delve into the key safety measures and precautions you should follow when working with jewelry-making tools, materials, and techniques.

Eye Protection

Safety Measure: When using tools that may produce debris or dust, such as grinders, drills, or files, wearing safety goggles or protective eyewear is vital to protect your eyes from potential hazards.
Rationale: Eye injuries are preventable with proper safety gear. Jewelry-making activities can generate tiny metal particles, dust, or debris that can cause eye irritation or injury if not adequately protected.

Ventilation

Safety Measure: Ensure adequate ventilation in your workspace, especially when engaging in jewelry-making processes that may release fumes, such as soldering or using chemicals.
Rationale: Proper ventilation helps to dissipate potentially harmful fumes, reducing your exposure to

noxious gasses and ensuring a safer and more comfortable working environment.

Handling Hazardous Materials

Safety Measure: Some materials used in jewelry making, such as pickling solutions or soldering flux, can be hazardous if not handled properly. Always follow recommended safety guidelines and use appropriate personal protective equipment (PPE) when working with these materials.
Rationale: Proper handling of hazardous materials minimizes health risks. It's crucial to read product labels and Material Safety Data Sheets (MSDS) to understand potential hazards and take precautions.

Fire Safety

Safety Measure: If your jewelry-making techniques involve open flames, like torch soldering, ensure you have fire safety equipment on hand, including a fire extinguisher and a fire blanket.
Rationale: Open flames pose a fire hazard. Having the right fire safety tools and knowing how to use them can prevent accidents and minimize damage in case of a fire.

Proper Tool Use and Maintenance

Safety Measure: Ensure that your tools are in good working condition and use them for their intended purposes. Follow safety guidelines for using tools such as hammers, saws, and mandrels.

Rationale: Using damaged or inappropriate tools can lead to accidents and injuries. Proper tool maintenance and safe usage practices are essential for your well-being.

Workspace Organization

Safety Measure: Keep your workspace organized, with tools and materials stored properly. Avoid clutter and ensure clear pathways in your workspace.
Rationale: An organized workspace is essential for efficiency and safety. It reduces the risk of accidents caused by tripping over materials or tools and allows you to focus on your projects without unnecessary distractions.

Personal Protective Equipment (PPE)

Safety Measure: Depending on the specific tasks and materials you work with, consider wearing PPE such as gloves, aprons, or respiratory protection to reduce the risk of exposure to hazards.
Rationale: PPE provides an extra layer of protection and minimizes contact with potentially harmful substances, ensuring your safety during jewelry-making processes.

First Aid Knowledge

Safety Measure: Familiarize yourself with basic first aid procedures and have a first aid kit readily available in your workspace.

Rationale: In case of minor injuries, having knowledge of first aid and the necessary supplies can make a significant difference in your safety and well-being.

Following these safety precautions in jewelry making is essential for safeguarding your health and well-being while enjoying your creative pursuits. Prioritizing safety ensures that your jewelry-making journey is both fulfilling and free from preventable accidents and health risks.

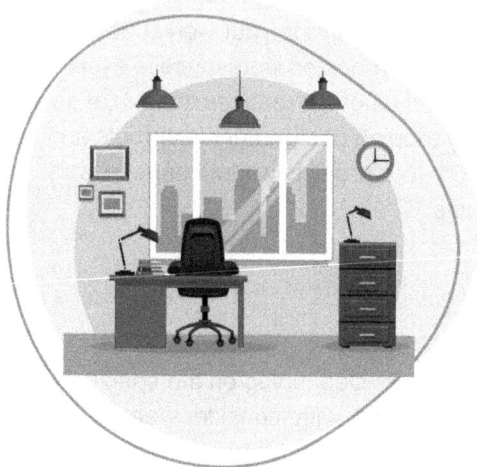

Setting Up Your Workspace

Setting up your jewelry-making workspace is a critical step in ensuring an efficient, comfortable, and safe environment for your creative endeavors. In this section, we'll explore the key elements of setting up your jewelry-making workspace, offering practical advice to help you create a space that onhances your productivity and enjoyment.

Organization

Importance: An organized workspace is essential for efficiency and creativity. Without a clutter-free environment, you may waste precious time searching for tools and materials, and distractions can disrupt your creative flow.

Recommendations

Invest in storage solutions such as drawers, containers, and shelves to keep tools, materials, and works-in-progress neatly organized.

Label containers and use a clear system for categorizing and storing materials. This makes it easy to find what you need quickly.

Lighting

Importance: Adequate lighting is crucial for working with small components and intricate details. Proper lighting ensures that you can see your work clearly and prevents eye strain.

Recommendations:

Install task lighting with adjustable fixtures that can be directed onto your workspace.

Consider using daylight-balanced LED lights to provide consistent and natural lighting.

Ergonomics

Importance: Jewelry making often involves hours of intricate work. Learning about ergonomics and setting up your workspace for comfort and safety is essential to reduce the risk of strain or injury, ensuring a comfortable and sustainable practice.

Recommendations:

Use an adjustable chair with good back support to maintain a comfortable posture.

Position your work table at a height that allows you to work with your arms and hands comfortably aligned with your work surface.

Place tools and materials within easy reach to minimize excessive stretching or straining.

Ventilation

Importance: Proper ventilation is crucial, especially when you're using processes that release fumes or dust, such as soldering or using chemicals.

Recommendations:

Work in a well-ventilated area or install a ventilation system like a fume extractor to remove potentially harmful fumes from your workspace.

Use a mask or respirator when working with materials or processes that generate airborne particles or fumes.

Safety Measures

Importance: Ensure that you have the necessary safety equipment and measures in place to protect yourself and prevent accidents.

Recommendations:

Have a fire extinguisher and a fire blanket readily available if you're using open flames or heat sources. Establish a clear and accessible area for first aid supplies and know how to use them in case of minor injuries.

Inspiration Zone

Importance: Your workspace should also inspire and motivate you. Personalize it with images, artwork, or objects that bring you joy and fuel your creativity.
Recommendations:
Create an "inspiration board" where you can pin images, quotes, or sketches that inspire your jewelry designs.
Surround yourself with your favorite jewelry pieces and creations to remind you of your artistic journey.

Workspace Maintenance

Importance: Regular maintenance of your workspace keeps it clean, safe, and conducive to creativity.
Recommendations:
Set aside time for regular cleaning and organization sessions to maintain an orderly workspace.
Periodically inspect your tools and equipment for signs of wear and tear, and perform necessary maintenance or replacements.

A well-organized, well-lit, and ergonomically designed workspace is the foundation for a successful and enjoyable jewelry-making practice. It not only enhances your creativity but also contributes to your safety and overall well-being. Tailoring your workspace to your specific needs and preferences ensures that you have a welcoming and efficient environment for your creative endeavors.

Chapter 2

Jewelry Design Fundamentals

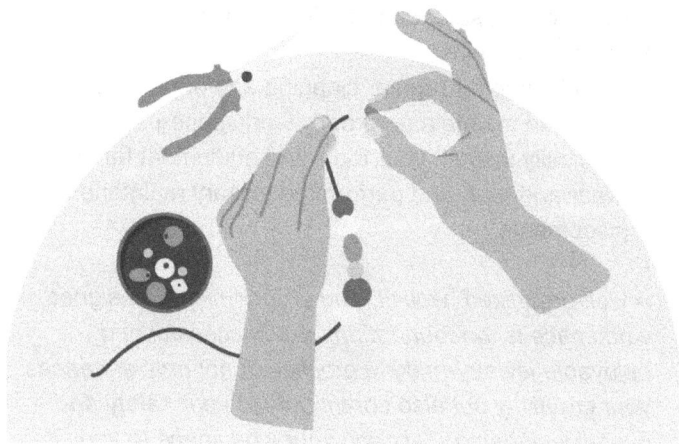

Chapter 2: Jewelry Design Fundamentals

In this chapter, we'll delve into the heart of jewelry making—design. Understanding the design fundamentals, exploring different styles, and discovering your unique aesthetic will provide you with the creative foundation needed to craft stunning, one-of-a-kind pieces.

The Importance of Design in Jewelry Making

Design is at the core of jewelry making, as it influences the overall aesthetics, appeal, and meaning of a piece. A well-designed piece of jewelry not only enhances its visual appeal but also conveys a story, sentiment, or artistic vision. Here, we'll explore the key elements and principles of design that are essential for creating compelling and harmonious jewelry.

Elements of Design

Line: The line is one of the most fundamental design elements in jewelry. It can be straight, curved, or a combination of both, and it forms the structure and shape of a piece. Consider the use of lines to create movement, balance, and visual interest in your designs.

Color: Color plays a crucial role in jewelry design, as it influences the emotional impact and overall aesthetic. Consider the color of gemstones, metals, and other materials to create harmonious or contrasting color schemes that convey different moods and emotions.

Shape: Shapes are the building blocks of design, and they can be organic or geometric. They define the form and structure of a piece. Experiment with various shapes, such as circles, ovals, triangles, or free-form shapes, to create visually appealing compositions.

Texture: Texture adds depth and tactile interest to your jewelry. Different surface treatments, like engraving, hammering, or etching, can create texture. The interplay of smooth and textured areas can create contrast and visual intrigue.

Space: Space refers to the areas around and within your jewelry design. How you use space can impact the overall composition. Balance the use of positive space (the jewelry itself) and negative space (the areas in between) to create a well-proportioned and aesthetically pleasing piece.

Pattern: Patterns are repetitions of elements in a design. Incorporating patterns, whether through gemstone placement, metalwork, or beading, can add visual rhythm and interest to your jewelry.

Principles of Design

Balance: Balance in design refers to the distribution of visual weight in a piece. Achieving balance can be through symmetry (formal balance) or asymmetry (informal balance), and it contributes to the overall harmony of your jewelry.

Proportion: Proportion involves the relative size and scale of elements within a design. Consider the size of gemstones, beads, and components to ensure they work together harmoniously.

Rhythm: Rhythm in design relates to the visual flow and movement within a piece. It can be achieved through repetition, alternation, or progression of elements. Rhythm adds a dynamic quality to your jewelry.

Emphasis: Emphasis highlights a focal point or center of interest in a design. This could be a prominent gemstone, a unique metalwork detail, or a specific color. Emphasis draws the viewer's eye and creates a visual focal point.

Unity: Unity in design ensures that all elements work together to create a cohesive and harmonious whole. The design should feel like a unified composition rather than a collection of disparate parts.

Design Inspiration

Nature: Nature is a rich source of design inspiration, offering an abundance of shapes, colors, and textures. Explore natural forms, from flowers and leaves to ocean waves and animal patterns, to infuse your jewelry with organic beauty.

Cultural Influences: Different cultures and traditions have their unique design motifs and symbols. Drawing from cultural influences can add depth and meaning to your jewelry, allowing you to tell stories or celebrate heritage.

Personal Stories: Your own experiences, memories, and emotions can serve as a wellspring of design inspiration. Consider creating pieces that convey your personal narratives or commemorate significant life events.

Art Movements: Art movements like Impressionism, Cubism, or Abstract Expressionism can inspire innovative and artistic jewelry designs. These movements often challenge conventions and encourage experimentation.

Fashion and Trends: Keeping an eye on current fashion trends and jewelry styles can provide insights into what's popular and in-demand. You can draw inspiration from contemporary styles to create pieces that resonate with modern tastes.

Understanding the elements and principles of design, seeking inspiration from various sources, and practicing the art of composition are essential aspects of jewelry design. By mastering these fundamentals, you'll be well-equipped to create jewelry that not only showcases your technical skill but also tells a compelling story and resonates with those who wear your creations. Design is the bridge between your imagination and the tangible beauty of your jewelry pieces.

Exploring Different Jewelry Styles

Jewelry design is a dynamic and ever-evolving field, influenced by cultural, historical, and artistic movements. Exploring different jewelry styles is a fascinating journey that allows you to draw inspiration from various periods, cultures, and design movements. Here, we'll take a closer look at some prominent jewelry styles, both historical and contemporary, to expand your design horizons:

Historical Styles

Ancient Civilizations:

Characteristics: Jewelry from ancient civilizations like Egypt, Greece, and Rome often featured intricate metalwork, gemstones, and symbolic motifs. These pieces were not only decorative but also carried cultural and religious significance. Influence: Explore the use of symbolism, ancient techniques, and culturally significant materials to create jewelry pieces inspired by these rich historical periods.

Art Nouveau:

Characteristics: Art Nouveau jewelry, popular in the late 19th and early 20th centuries, is known for its flowing, organic forms inspired by nature, including intricate floral and insect motifs. The use of enamel, plique-à-jour, and malleable metals is prevalent. Influence: Capture the essence of nature and organic forms in your designs. Experiment with enameling techniques and delicate metalwork to pay homage to the Art Nouveau movement.

Art Deco:

Characteristics: Art Deco jewelry emerged in the 1920s and 1930s, characterized by bold geometric shapes, symmetrical patterns, and the use of

gemstones like diamonds, emeralds, and onyx. This style exuded luxury and modernity.
Influence: Embrace the sleek and geometric aesthetics of Art Deco by incorporating bold shapes, contrasting colors, and high-quality gemstones into your designs.

Victorian Era:

Characteristics: The Victorian era produced a wide range of jewelry styles, from sentimental lockets and mourning jewelry to elaborate, gem-studded pieces. Sentimentality, intricate detailing, and the use of different materials were hallmarks of this era.
Influence: Draw inspiration from Victorian-era romanticism, symbolism, and intricate metalwork. Incorporate lockets, cameos, and symbolic elements into your jewelry creations.

Contemporary Styles

Minimalist:

Characteristics: Minimalist jewelry is characterized by simplicity, clean lines, and a focus on essential forms. It often features geometric shapes, understated materials, and a "less is more" approach.
Influence: Embrace simplicity and elegance in your designs. Use minimalistic forms and high-quality materials to create pieces that convey a sense of sophistication and timeless appeal.

Bohemian:

Characteristics: Bohemian jewelry exudes a free-spirited and eclectic vibe, often incorporating natural elements like feathers, leather, and semi-precious stones. Layering and mixing different textures and materials are common.
Influence: Experiment with a mix of materials and textures, combining metals, beads, and organic elements to create jewelry that embodies the Bohemian spirit.

Vintage:

Characteristics: Vintage-inspired jewelry draws from various historical periods and often incorporates filigree, ornate settings, and vintage-style gem cuts. It celebrates the elegance and nostalgia of bygone eras.
Influence: Explore the aesthetics of different vintage periods and incorporate vintage elements like filigree, cameos, and old-world charm into your designs.

High Fashion:

Characteristics: High fashion jewelry is bold, extravagant, and often serves as a statement piece. It frequently features oversized gemstones, unique materials, and avant-garde designs.

Influence: Push the boundaries of design by creating bold, avant-garde jewelry that reflects your artistic vision and makes a striking statement.

By exploring and embracing these different jewelry styles, you can expand your design repertoire and find inspiration from various artistic movements and time periods. Whether you're drawn to the timeless elegance of Art Deco, the organic beauty of Art Nouveau, or the free-spirited charm of Bohemian jewelry, each style offers a unique canvas for your creativity and self-expression.

Finding Your Unique Design Aesthetic

Developing a unique design aesthetic is a fundamental aspect of becoming a successful jewelry designer. Your aesthetic sets your work apart, defines your signature style, and can become a powerful branding tool. Here, we'll delve into the process of discovering and honing your unique design aesthetic:

1. Self-Reflection and Inspiration:

    Self-Reflection: Start by reflecting on your personal tastes, values, and experiences. Consider what colors, shapes, and themes resonate with you on a deeper level. Your jewelry should be an extension of your personality and interests.

Inspiration Sources: Draw inspiration from various sources, including art, nature, culture, and personal experiences. Explore different materials, gemstones, and techniques to see what ignites your creative spark.

2. Experimentation and Exploration:

Try New Techniques: Don't be afraid to experiment with various jewelry-making techniques. Wire wrapping, metalworking, beading, and enameling are just a few of the many possibilities. Experimentation allows you to discover what techniques you enjoy and excel at.

Explore Materials: Jewelry can be crafted from a wide range of materials, from precious metals and gemstones to recycled or upcycled components. Experiment with different materials to see which ones resonate with your style.

3. Develop a Signature Element:

Identify a specific element that sets your jewelry apart. It could be a unique gemstone setting, a particular wirework pattern, or a distinctive color palette. Developing a signature element helps your work become recognizable and memorable.

4. Consistency and Cohesion:

Strive for consistency and cohesion in your designs. Your jewelry pieces should form a cohesive collection that tells a story or conveys a specific theme or aesthetic. This helps create a strong brand identity.

5. Feedback and Evaluation:

   Seek feedback from peers, mentors, or customers. Constructive feedback can provide valuable insights into how your designs are perceived and where improvements can be made. It also helps you refine your aesthetic.

6. Stay Open to Evolution:

   Be open to the evolution of your aesthetic. As you gain experience and exposure to new influences, your design style may naturally evolve. Don't feel constrained by an initial design aesthetic if you feel the need to explore new directions.

7. Market Research and Trends:

   Keep an eye on market trends and customer preferences. While your unique aesthetic is your primary focus, understanding market demands can help you align your designs with what's in demand.

8. Storytelling and Branding:

   Develop a narrative for your brand and your jewelry pieces. Your jewelry should tell a story, whether it's about your inspiration, your creative process, or the significance of a particular piece. Effective branding can help convey your unique aesthetic to your audience.

9. Create a Portfolio:

    Build a portfolio of your work that showcases your unique aesthetic. Whether it's through a website, social media, or physical displays, your portfolio is a visual representation of your design style.

10. Celebrate Uniqueness:

    Embrace what makes your designs unique. Don't be afraid to push the boundaries of conventional jewelry design and celebrate the quirks, imperfections, and distinctive elements that set your work apart.

Finding and nurturing your unique design aesthetic is an ongoing journey. It's a process of self-discovery and artistic growth that evolves over time. Your unique aesthetic is what makes your jewelry a reflection of your creativity, personality, and artistic vision. It's the essence of what sets your work apart in a crowded and competitive market, and it's the key to creating jewelry that resonates with your customers and brings you artistic fulfillment.

Sketching and Planning Your Jewelry Designs

Sketching and planning are essential steps in the jewelry design process. They serve as the blueprint for transforming your creative vision into tangible, wearable pieces of art. In this section, we'll explore the significance of sketching and planning in jewelry design and provide practical guidance on how to go about it.

The Importance of Sketching and Planning

Visualization: Sketching allows you to visualize your design ideas. It's a way to bring your imagination to life on paper. By sketching, you can see the proportions, shapes, and overall composition of your jewelry before you begin the physical crafting process.

Communication: Sketches serve as a means of communication. Whether you're working on your designs independently or collaborating with clients, colleagues, or manufacturers, a clear and detailed sketch can convey your intentions effectively.

Problem-Solving: During the sketching phase, you can identify potential design issues or challenges before investing time and materials in the actual creation. It's an opportunity to refine and troubleshoot your ideas.

Creativity and Exploration: Sketching allows for creative exploration. You can try out different variations of a design, experiment with new elements, and refine your concept until you're satisfied with the result.

Steps for Effective Sketching and Planning

Gather Inspiration:
Start by collecting sources of inspiration. These can be photographs, nature, art, architecture, or even emotions and personal experiences. Inspiration is the fuel for your creative process.

Materials and Tools:
Invest in quality sketching materials such as sketchbooks, pencils, erasers, rulers, and fine-tipped pens. A sketchbook is a dedicated space for your design ideas.

Doodle and Brainstorm:
Begin with loose doodles and brainstorming. Allow your ideas to flow freely without self-critique. This is the stage for generating as many ideas as possible.

Refinement:
Select the most promising concepts from your initial sketches and refine them. Add details, make adjustments, and consider the practical aspects of turning your idea into a wearable piece.

Technical Details:
Pay attention to technical aspects such as dimensions, materials, and techniques. This information will guide you during the actual crafting process.

Color Rendering (if applicable):
If your jewelry design involves specific colors, consider creating color renderings to bring the design to life. This can be especially useful for pieces with gemstones or intricate enamel work.

Annotation:
Annotate your sketches with notes or labels to clarify your design intent. Describe the materials, gemstones, or specific techniques you plan to use.

Multiple Views:
For complex pieces, it's beneficial to sketch multiple views. Show the front, side, and back views of your jewelry to ensure a comprehensive understanding of the design.

Feedback and Revision:
Seek feedback from peers, mentors, or clients. Their input can provide fresh perspectives and help you make

improvements. Don't hesitate to revise your sketches based on feedback.

Prototyping:
In some cases, creating a prototype or a 3D model of your design can provide a more tangible understanding of how the jewelry will look and feel. Prototyping is especially valuable for intricate or custom pieces.

Keep a Design Journal:
Maintain a design journal or sketchbook to document your design journey. This can be a valuable resource for tracking your creative process and revisiting past ideas.

Sketching and planning are integral parts of the jewelry design process. They provide a structured framework for transforming your imaginative concepts into beautiful, wearable pieces of art. Whether you're a professional jeweler or an enthusiast, effective sketching and planning help ensure that your designs are well-thought-out, visually pleasing, and aligned with your creative vision.

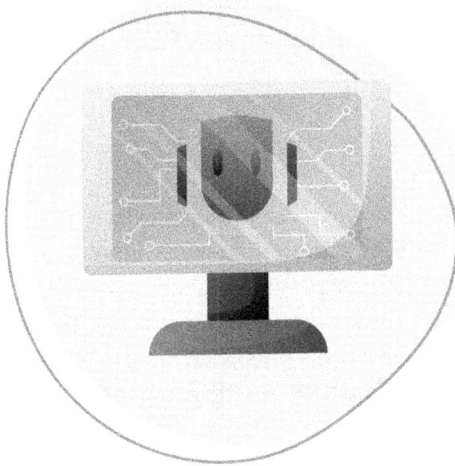

Using AI to Help Generate Ideas

The integration of artificial intelligence (AI) into the creative process of jewelry design represents a fascinating and innovative approach. AI can serve as a valuable tool for generating design ideas, assisting designers in exploring new possibilities, and enhancing the overall design process. Here, we'll explore the ways in which AI can be used to aid in the generation of jewelry design ideas:

1. Design Inspiration:

AI algorithms can be programmed to analyze vast databases of images, artwork, and jewelry designs. By leveraging machine learning, AI can identify patterns, trends, and common elements in various design styles.

Jewelry designers can use AI-powered tools to explore a wide range of design inspirations from historical styles to contemporary trends.

2. Customization and Personalization:

AI can assist in creating personalized jewelry designs tailored to individual preferences. By inputting parameters such as gemstone choices, metal types, and design themes, AI can generate unique design concepts that align with the client's specific tastes. This level of customization enhances the client's engagement with the design process.

3. Design Optimization:

AI can analyze and optimize designs for various factors, including cost-effectiveness, structural integrity, and aesthetic appeal. AI algorithms can assess how different materials and techniques impact the final design, allowing designers to make informed decisions.

4. Quick Iteration:

AI enables rapid iteration and exploration of design variations. Designers can input initial ideas into AI systems, which can then generate multiple design options, helping them visualize the potential directions a design can take. This expedites the ideation process and provides a broader spectrum of design choices.

5. Design Validation:

AI can assist in validating the feasibility and integrity of a design. By simulating wear and tear, stress points, and durability, AI can identify potential issues and suggest modifications to enhance the longevity and functionality of the jewelry piece.

6. Market Trends Analysis:

AI can monitor and analyze market trends and customer preferences. By tracking what styles and features are currently in demand, designers can use AI-driven insights to adapt their designs and align them with market trends.

7. Color Palettes and Material Suggestions:

AI can recommend color palettes and material combinations based on design objectives, the intended wearer, and market trends. This can help designers make informed decisions about which materials and color schemes to use in their creations.

8. Collaboration and Crowd-Sourcing:

AI-powered platforms can facilitate collaborative design efforts by connecting designers from around the world. Designers can collectively work on a project, benefiting from diverse perspectives and ideas.

9. Intellectual Property Protection:

AI can assist in identifying potential copyright or trademark issues by scanning existing designs and comparing them to the one being developed. This helps designers ensure that their creations are original and do not infringe on existing intellectual property.

10. Cost Estimation and Budgeting:

AI can provide cost estimates for jewelry designs by considering factors such as materials, labor, and overhead. This information can assist designers in making budget-conscious decisions while maintaining the desired quality.

The use of AI in jewelry design is an exciting and evolving field. By leveraging AI tools and platforms, designers can enhance their creative process, save time, and explore innovative ideas more efficiently. AI serves as a complementary tool, offering a fresh perspective and assisting in the ideation phase, ultimately empowering designers to bring their imaginative visions to life in a more informed and efficient manner.

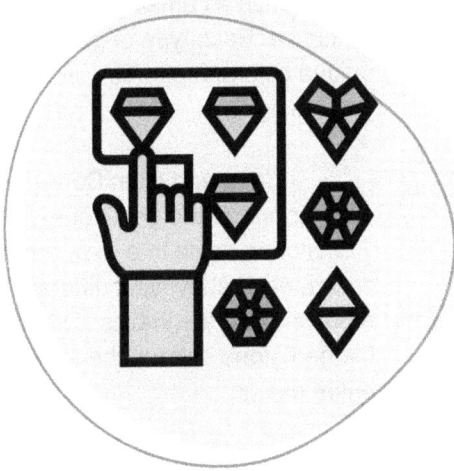

Selecting Gemstones and Materials

The selection of gemstones and materials is a pivotal step in the jewelry design process. Gemstones and materials not only contribute to the visual appeal of the jewelry but also play a significant role in the design's overall aesthetics, durability, and value. Here, we'll explore the art of choosing gemstones and materials for your jewelry designs:

    1. Gemstones:

        Type of Gemstones: The choice of gemstones is a central design decision. You'll need to decide between precious stones like diamonds, sapphires, and rubies, or semi-precious stones such as amethyst, topaz, or turquoise. Each type of gemstone brings unique colors, properties, and value to your design.

Color and Hue: Consider the color or hue of the gemstone. Gemstones come in a wide array of colors, each conveying different emotions and aesthetics. The color of the gemstone can set the tone for your entire design.

Shape and Cut: The shape and cut of a gemstone influence the design's style and aesthetics. Round, oval, pear, and marquise cuts, among others, offer diverse design possibilities.

Size and Carat Weight: The size of the gemstone affects the overall balance and proportions of the jewelry. Consider how the gemstone size complements the design and the wearer's preferences.

Clarity and Inclusions: The clarity of a gemstone is an important factor. It's about the presence or absence of inclusions or imperfections within the stone. A higher clarity rating usually results in a more valuable gem.

Durability and Hardness: Different gemstones have varying levels of hardness and durability. For pieces that will be worn daily, durability is crucial to ensure the gemstone remains intact and unscathed.

Budget Considerations: The cost of gemstones can vary significantly. Consider your budget and whether you want to invest in precious stones or explore more cost-effective alternatives.

2. Metals:

Type of Metal: The choice of metal for your jewelry piece significantly impacts its aesthetic and durability. Common metals used in jewelry making include gold (in various colors), silver, platinum, and alternative metals like titanium.

Metal Purity: Different alloys and purity levels are available for metals like gold. For example, 24-karat gold is pure gold, while 18-karat gold is mixed with other metals for strength and durability. Purity affects the color and durability of the metal.

Color of Metal: The color of the metal can be a design feature in itself. White gold, rose gold, and yellow gold offer different aesthetic possibilities. Consider how the metal color complements the gemstone and design.

Texture and Finish: The texture and finish of the metal, such as high polish, matte, brushed, or textured surfaces, add depth and character to the design.

Hypoallergenic Considerations: Some people have allergies to specific metals, like nickel. If you're designing for a wide audience, consider using hypoallergenic metals.

3. Additional Materials:

Beads and Gemstone Chips: Beads and gemstone chips can add texture and color to your designs. They are popular in beading and stringing projects.

Cords and Chains: The type of cord or chain used affects the design's style and functionality. Choices range from delicate chains to leather cords and more.

Accents and Findings: Clasps, spacers, and other findings contribute to the jewelry's functionality and aesthetics. Select findings that complement the overall design.

Eco-Friendly and Sustainable Materials: With growing interest in sustainability, consider using eco-friendly materials like recycled metals and ethically sourced gemstones.

Resin and Enamel: These materials can add color, depth, and protection to your designs. They're often used to encapsulate small objects or create vibrant, eye-catching elements.

Alternative Materials: Think beyond traditional materials. Experiment with materials like wood, ceramics, or acrylic for unique and unconventional designs.

When selecting gemstones and materials for your jewelry designs, it's essential to strike a balance between aesthetics, durability, and budget. Your choices play a crucial role in realizing your design vision, and they have a significant impact on the final piece's visual appeal and market value. Careful consideration of these factors ensures that your jewelry design is not only visually stunning but also functional and meaningful.

Chapter 3

Jewelry Making Techniques

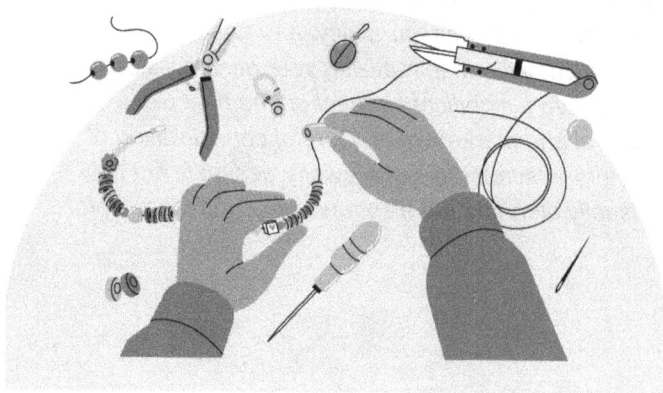

Chapter 3: Jewelry Making Techniques

In this chapter, we transition from the conceptual phase of jewelry design to the practical phase of bringing your designs to life. Jewelry making techniques are the hands-on skills and methods that transform your ideas into wearable art. This chapter explores various techniques and processes essential for crafting beautiful jewelry.

Introduction to Jewelry Making Techniques

Jewelry-making techniques are the building blocks of your creative process. These techniques encompass a diverse array of skills and methods used to transform raw materials into wearable works of art. Understanding and practicing these techniques will enable you to craft beautiful, unique pieces that reflect your style and vision.

Wire Wrapping

Wire wrapping is a versatile and accessible jewelry-making technique that involves shaping and securing wire to create intricate designs and settings for gemstones and beads. Here's what you need to know:

Basic Wire Wrapping: Learn the fundamental techniques for creating wire loops, wrapped loops, and simple designs.

Advanced Wire Wrapping: Progress to more complex designs, such as wire-wrapped pendants, intricate wire weaves, and filigree work.

Materials: Explore the various types of wire, such as copper, sterling silver, and gold-filled wire, and choose the one that best suits your design.

Tools: Gather the essential tools for wire wrapping, including pliers, wire cutters, and mandrels.

Beading and Stringing

Beading and stringing are popular techniques for creating jewelry using beads of various materials, shapes, and sizes. Key considerations include:

Bead Types: Explore the vast world of beads, from glass and crystal to gemstone, seed beads, and pearls.

Stringing Materials: Choose suitable stringing materials like wire, thread, cord, or chain to hold your beads together.

Design Principles: Understand design principles such as pattern, balance, and color to create visually appealing beadwork.

Clasps and Findings: Learn how to attach clasps and findings to complete your beaded jewelry.

Metalworking

Metalworking is a broad technique that includes a variety of processes for shaping, forming, and finishing metal elements in your jewelry:

Soldering: Master the art of soldering to join metal components seamlessly. This technique is crucial for creating metal jewelry.

Texturing and Patina: Experiment with texturing techniques to add unique surface patterns to your metal pieces. Patination methods can create beautiful antique effects.

Metal Clay: Explore the world of metal clay, a malleable material that can be molded and fired to create intricate metal designs.

Etching and Engraving: Learn how to etch and engrave metal for personalized and detailed designs.

Polymer Clay Creations

Polymer clay is a versatile medium that allows you to create colorful and detailed jewelry components:

Clay Basics: Understand the properties of polymer clay, its curing process, and color mixing.

Canes and Millefiori: Discover techniques for creating intricate canes and millefiori patterns, which are perfect for beads and pendants.

Sculpting and Modeling: Learn how to sculpt and model polymer clay into 3D shapes and designs.

Baking and Finishing: Master the baking and finishing processes to create durable and polished polymer clay jewelry.

Resin and Glass Work

Resin and glass are materials that add depth and shine to your jewelry. Here's what you can explore:

Resin Basics: Understand the different types of resin and how to mix, pour, and cure it for various jewelry applications.

Inclusions: Experiment with adding inclusions like dried flowers, glitter, or small objects to your resin jewelry for a unique look.

Glass Techniques: Delve into glass work, including techniques like glass fusing, lampworking, and stained glass, to create intricate glass components.

Etching and Enamel: Explore methods for etching and enameling glass to add texture and color.

Advanced Techniques and Tips

As you gain experience in jewelry making, you can push your creative boundaries with advanced techniques and tips:

Stone Setting: Master stone setting techniques, such as bezel, prong, and channel settings, for incorporating gemstones into your designs.

Enameling: Explore advanced enameling techniques, including cloisonné and champlevé, for intricate designs.

Mixed Media: Combine various techniques, materials, and artistic forms to create truly unique and innovative pieces.

Troubleshooting: Learn common troubleshooting tips to overcome challenges that may arise during the jewelry-making process.

Mastering jewelry-making techniques is a continuous journey, and each technique opens new possibilities for your creative expression. Whether you're drawn to wire wrapping, beading, metalworking, polymer clay, resin, glass, or advanced methods, these techniques are the building blocks of your jewelry-making skills. By mastering them, you'll be well-equipped to craft stunning, one-of-a-kind jewelry pieces that reflect your artistic vision and style.

Chapter 4

Tools and Equipment

Chapter 4: Tools and Equipment

A fundamental aspect of jewelry making is having the right tools and equipment at your disposal. In this chapter, we'll delve into the essential tools required, specialized equipment for advanced techniques, and how to maintain and care for your tools to ensure they remain in optimal working condition.

Overview of Essential Jewelry-Making Tools

The foundation of every jewelry maker's toolkit consists of essential tools used for various tasks. Here's an overview of these key tools:

Pliers: Pliers are versatile tools used for bending, shaping, gripping, and holding various jewelry components. The most common types include chain-nose, round-nose, flat-nose, and bent-nose pliers.

Wire Cutters: Wire cutters are designed to cleanly cut metal wire, beading wire, and other stringing materials. They come in various sizes to accommodate different gauges of wire.

Jeweler's Saw: A jeweler's saw is used for precision cutting of metal sheet, wire, and other materials. It allows for intricate and detailed designs.

Files: Files are essential for smoothing and shaping metal edges and surfaces. They come in various shapes and sizes, including needle files for fine detail work.

Mandrels: Mandrels are cylindrical or cone-shaped tools used for shaping rings, bracelets, and other circular jewelry components. They are available in steel, wood, and plastic.

Hammer: A jeweler's hammer is used for tasks like flattening metal, texturing, and forging. Various hammerheads offer different textures and effects.

Calipers: Calipers are used to measure and verify the dimensions of jewelry components accurately.

Bench Block: A bench block provides a sturdy surface for hammering and shaping metal without damaging your work surface or tools.

Bezel Pusher and Roller: These tools are used for securing gemstones and cabochons in bezel settings.

Third Hand: A third hand is a tool with adjustable arms and clips that securely holds small components during soldering and other tasks.

Soldering Equipment: Soldering tools include a torch, solder, flux, and a soldering pick, used for joining metal components. Safety gear like fire-resistant surface, heat-resistant gloves, and safety goggles are essential when soldering,

Safety Gear: Safety goggles, dust masks, and proper ventilation are crucial for protecting your eyes and respiratory system when working with metal, chemicals, or power tools.

Specialized Equipment for Advanced Techniques

As you advance in your jewelry-making skills, you may require specialized equipment for specific techniques. Some of these advanced tools include:

Flex Shaft: A flex shaft is a versatile, high-speed rotary tool used for tasks like polishing, engraving, drilling, and more. It comes with various attachments and accessories.

Lapidary Equipment: Lapidary tools, such as a cabbing machine or a lapidary wheel, are used for shaping and polishing gemstones and minerals.

Casting Equipment: Casting tools are required for the lost-wax casting process, allowing you to create intricate metal jewelry pieces.

Enameling Kiln: If you're delving into enamel work, a kiln is necessary for fusing powdered glass to metal surfaces.

Glass Torch: Lampworking or glass bead making requires a specialized glass torch for shaping and working with glass rods.

Metal Forming Equipment: Advanced metalworking may involve hydraulic presses, rolling mills, and power hammers for shaping metal.

Ultrasonic Cleaner: An ultrasonic cleaner is useful for quickly and thoroughly cleaning jewelry components, removing debris and residues.

Maintenance and Care of Your Tools

To ensure the longevity and functionality of your tools, it's important to practice proper maintenance and care:

Cleaning: Regularly clean your tools, removing dirt, grease, and debris. Use appropriate cleaning solutions and lubricants for moving parts.

Storage: Store your tools in a dry, clean, and organized environment to prevent rust and damage. Invest in tool organizers, cabinets, or wall-mounted racks.

Sharpening: Keep cutting tools, like saw blades and file edges, sharp for precise and efficient work. Sharpening stones and files can be used for this purpose.

Replacement Parts: For tools with replaceable parts, keep extra components on hand to swiftly replace worn or damaged pieces.

Proper Use: Follow the manufacturer's guidelines for each tool and use them for their intended purpose to prevent unnecessary wear and tear.

Preventative Maintenance: Periodically inspect your tools for signs of wear or damage, addressing issues promptly to avoid further deterioration.

By understanding the essential jewelry-making tools, acquiring specialized equipment for advanced techniques, and practicing diligent maintenance and care, you'll have a well-equipped workspace and extend the life of your tools, ensuring that they remain reliable for your creative endeavors. These tools are the artisans' companions in crafting exquisite jewelry, and their proper handling is essential for your jewelry-making journey.

Chapter 5

Mastering Basic Jewelry-Making Projects

Chapter 5: Mastering Basic Jewelry-Making Projects

In this chapter, we delve into hands-on jewelry making projects that allow you to apply the techniques and skills you've learned. These projects serve as building blocks for your jewelry-making journey, helping you gain confidence and mastery in the craft.

Creating Simple Earrings

Earrings are a great starting point for beginners. Here's an overview of how to create simple, yet elegant, earrings:

Materials and Tools: Begin with basic materials like beads, wire, and earring hooks. You'll need pliers, wire cutters, and round-nose pliers.

Design Considerations: Choose a design that suits your style, whether it's dainty studs, dangling earrings, or hoops. Consider the color and type of beads or gemstones to create your desired look.

Assembly: Cut the wire to the desired length, create loops, and attach beads. Use techniques like wire wrapping or bead stringing to complete the earring.

Finishing: Attach earring hooks and ensure a secure closure. Polish the finished earrings to achieve a professional look.

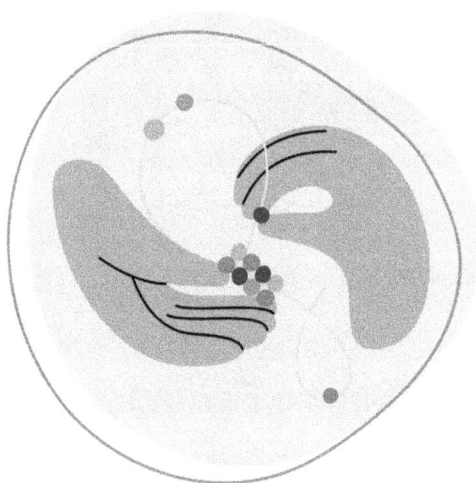

Making Bracelets

Bracelets offer versatility in design and provide a canvas for creativity. Here's an outline of the process:

Materials and Tools: Gather beads, wire, cord, or chain. Pliers, cutters, and clasps are essential tools.

Design Considerations: Choose a bracelet style, such as bangles, cuffs, or charm bracelets. Decide on bead patterns and colors to match your vision.

Assembly: String beads or attach them to wire or chain. Use crimp beads or knots to secure them in place. Create closures like lobster clasps or toggle clasps.

Finishing: Ensure that the bracelet is the right length and comfortable to wear. Check for any sharp edges or rough spots. A professional finish is key to a polished piece.

Designing Necklaces

Necklaces can be both statement pieces and subtle adornments. Here's how to craft a necklace:

Materials and Tools: Choose a chain, cord, or wire, along with beads, pendants, or focal elements. Pliers, cutters, and clasps are necessary.

Design Considerations: Decide on the necklace's length and style, such as chokers, princess, or opera length. Coordinate the choice of materials with your design concept.

Assembly: String beads or attach pendants, ensuring even spacing and balance. Use crimps or knots to secure components. Incorporate findings and closures.

Finishing: Assess the necklace's comfort and aesthetics. Make adjustments as needed, and ensure that the closure is secure and user-friendly.

Crafting Rings

Creating rings allows you to work on smaller-scale jewelry projects. Here's how to make custom rings:

Materials and Tools: You'll need wire or metal sheet for the ring band, as well as gemstones or decorative elements. Pliers, mandrels, and hammers are useful tools.

Design Considerations: Determine the ring size, style, and design. Consider whether you want a simple band or a statement piece with gemstone accents.

Assembly: Shape the ring band according to the desired size and style. Add any embellishments or gemstones, ensuring they're secure. Soldering may be required for certain designs.

Finishing: Polish the ring to a high shine or apply a desired finish. Ensure the fit is comfortable and that any stones are securely set.

Customizing Jewelry with Personal Touches

Personalizing your jewelry adds sentimental value. Here are ways to incorporate personal touches:

Initials and Names: Engrave initials, names, or special dates on metal components or pendants.

Birthstones: Use birthstones to represent loved ones, creating jewelry that tells a unique story.

Handwriting or Messages: Capture handwritten notes or messages in jewelry through techniques like engraving or resin casting.

Photo Jewelry: Embed tiny photos in resin or create photo lockets to keep cherished memories close.

Memento Jewelry: Incorporate small mementos, such as dried flowers, into rooin or metal settings to preserve memories.

By mastering these basic jewelry projects and adding personal touches, you'll develop your skills and create meaningful, personalized pieces that reflect your creativity and style. These projects provide a strong foundation for exploring more complex and intricate jewelry designs as you continue your journey in the craft of jewelry making.

Chapter 6

Quality and Craftsmanship

Chapter 6: Quality and Craftsmanship

In this chapter, we explore the importance of quality and craftsmanship in jewelry making. Creating high-quality jewelry goes beyond aesthetics; it encompasses precision, durability, and ethical considerations. Here's an in-depth look at the various aspects covered in this chapter:

Achieving High-Quality Jewelry

Crafting high-quality jewelry is a testament to your skills and dedication. Here's how to ensure your jewelry meets the highest standards:

Materials Selection: Begin with top-quality materials. Choose metals like 18K gold or 925 silver, and source gemstones with excellent clarity and color.

Precision and Detail: Pay attention to precision in every aspect of your work, from stone setting to soldering. Detailed craftsmanship ensures a professional finish.

Durability: High-quality jewelry is built to withstand everyday wear. Ensure that findings, clasps, and connections are secure and durable.

Polishing and Finish: Achieve a flawless finish by using proper polishing techniques. A well-polished piece not only looks beautiful but also feels smooth and comfortable to wear.

Ethical Considerations: Consider the ethical aspects of your materials and processes. Ethical sourcing of gemstones and metals, as well as environmentally responsible practices, adds to the quality of your jewelry.

Quality Control and Inspection

Implementing quality control measures is vital to ensure consistency and excellence in your jewelry pieces. Key points include:

Inspection Checklist: Develop a checklist to inspect each piece thoroughly. This checklist may cover aspects like stone settings, symmetry, surface finish, and overall aesthetics.

Testing: Use testing methods to verify the authenticity of materials. For instance, use acid tests to confirm the karat of gold or verify gemstone authenticity with gemological testing.

Work Environment: Maintain a clean, organized workspace to reduce the risk of errors and contamination. Proper lighting and magnification tools aid in detailed inspections.

Feedback Loop: Continuously improve by gathering feedback from customers and peers. Constructive criticism helps refine your craftsmanship.

Documentation: Keep detailed records of your materials, processes, and inspections. Documentation aids in tracing the quality of each piece and can be valuable for future reference.

Working with Precious Metals and Gemstones

Crafting jewelry with precious metals and gemstones requires specialized knowledge. Here's how to work with these materials:

Metal Selection: Precious metals like gold, platinum, and silver have unique properties. Understand their characteristics and choose the right metal for your design.

Gemstone Knowledge: Study the properties of gemstones, including hardness, durability, and sensitivity to heat or chemicals. This knowledge guides proper care and setting techniques.

Stone Setting: Master stone setting techniques, such as prong settings, bezel settings, and pave settings. Precise stone setting ensures gemstones are securely held and aligned.

Casting and Alloying: Learn about casting processes and alloying to create custom metal blends. This knowledge allows you to control the metal's characteristics and appearance.

Setting Techniques: Explore advanced setting techniques like channel setting, flush setting, and bead setting for different styles and designs.

Sustainable Jewelry Making Practices

The jewelry industry is increasingly moving towards sustainability and ethical practices. Here's how you can contribute to sustainability in your jewelry making:

Ethical Sourcing: Choose responsibly sourced materials, including conflict-free diamonds and Fair Trade metals.

Recycled Metals: Consider working with recycled metals to reduce the environmental impact of mining.

Eco-Friendly Processes: Adopt eco-friendly jewelry-making processes, such as using non-toxic chemicals and implementing recycling and waste reduction practices.

Artisanal and Small-Scale Mining Support: Support artisanal miners and small-scale mining initiatives that follow ethical and sustainable practices.

Consumer Education: Educate your customers about the importance of ethical and sustainable jewelry, making them more conscious consumers.

Quality and craftsmanship are at the heart of the jewelry-making process. By striving for the highest quality in your work, conducting thorough quality control, understanding the intricacies of precious materials, and embracing sustainable practices, you not only create beautiful jewelry but also contribute to the overall integrity and ethical standards of the jewelry industry.

Chapter 7

Jewelry Pricing and Costing

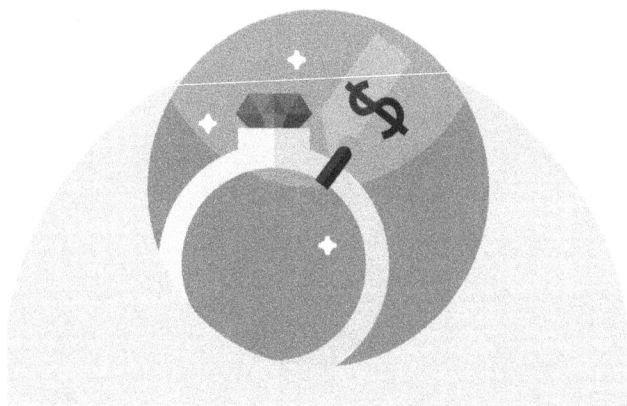

Chapter 7: Jewelry Pricing and Costing

Jewelry pricing and costing is a critical aspect of running a successful jewelry-making business. In this chapter, we explore the methods and strategies for determining the right prices for your jewelry pieces, ensuring that you cover your costs, make a profit, and remain competitive in the market.

Determining the Cost of Materials

To price your jewelry accurately, you must start by calculating the cost of materials. Here's how to do it:

1. Materials Inventory: Keep a detailed record of the materials used in each piece, including metals, gemstones, beads, and findings.

2. Supplier Costs: Consider the purchase price of materials from your suppliers, including shipping fees and taxes.

3. Wastage: Factor in the percentage of materials that may be wasted or damaged during the production process.

4. Consumables: Include costs for any consumables used in production, such as solder, adhesive, and polishing compounds.

5. Research: Regularly research material prices to stay updated and adjust your pricing accordingly.

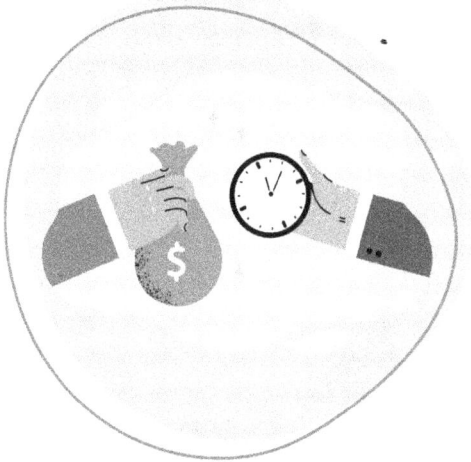

Factoring in Labor and Time

Your time and labor are valuable and must be accounted for when pricing your jewelry:

1. Hourly Rate: Determine your hourly labor rate based on your experience, skills, and market rates. Consider the time spent on design, assembly, stone setting, and finishing.

2. Time Tracking: Keep accurate records of the time spent on each piece, from the initial concept to the final finishing touches.

3. Overheads: Include overhead costs, such as studio rent, utilities, and maintenance, as part of your labor cost.

97

4. Efficiency: Continuously improve your efficiency and production processes to reduce labor costs.

Pricing Strategies for Profit

To make a profit and ensure your jewelry business is sustainable, consider the following pricing strategies:

1. Keystone Pricing: Double the cost of materials and labor to determine the wholesale price. Then, double the wholesale price to establish the retail price.

2. Market Research: Analyze your target market and competitors to set competitive prices while maintaining profitability,

3. Value-Based Pricing: Price your jewelry based on the perceived value it offers to customers. Consider the uniqueness of your designs, craftsmanship, and any additional services you provide.

4. Tiered Pricing: Offer different price points within your product range, catering to a variety of customer budgets.

5. Discounts and Sales: Plan occasional sales and discounts to attract more customers and clear inventory.

Competitor Analysis

Understanding your competition is crucial for effective pricing. Here's how to conduct competitor analysis:

1. Market Research: Study the offerings of your direct competitors, noting their pricing strategies, design styles, and customer base.

2. Unique Selling Proposition (USP): Identify what sets your jewelry apart from competitors. Emphasize your USP in marketing and pricing strategies.

3. Pricing Comparison: Compare your prices with competitors. Consider whether you want to position your jewelry as more affordable, premium, or somewhere in between.

4. Customer Feedback: Collect feedback from your customers and potential clients to better understand their preferences and expectations regarding pricing.

Setting Realistic Price Points

To ensure your jewelry is not only priced competitively but also sustainably, focus on these factors:

1. Profit Margin: Calculate a reasonable profit margin that covers your costs, provides income, and allows for business growth.

2. Customer Perceived Value: Your pricing should align with the perceived value of your jewelry in the eyes of your target market.

3. Testing and Adjusting: Be open to testing different price points and adjusting them based on customer responses and market conditions.

4. Transparency: Communicate your pricing clearly to customers, explaining the value they receive for their investment.

Pricing your jewelry accurately is a balancing act between covering costs, ensuring profitability, and meeting market expectations. By factoring in material costs, labor, and overheads, employing effective pricing strategies, conducting competitor analysis, and setting realistic price points, you can run a successful jewelry-making business that thrives in the competitive market.

.

Chapter 8

Building Your Brand

Chapter 8: Building Your Brand

Building a strong and distinctive brand is a key aspect of a successful jewelry business. In this chapter, we will explore various elements and strategies for establishing and promoting your brand identity.

Branding Your Jewelry Business

Your brand is more than just a name or a logo; it's the perception and emotions that customers associate with your business. Here's how to start building your brand:

1. Brand Identity: Define what your brand represents, including its values, mission, and vision. What kind of jewelry do you create, and

what makes it special? Understand the essence of your brand.

2. Target Audience: Identify your target market, their preferences, and needs. Knowing your audience helps tailor your brand to appeal to them.

3. Differentiation: Determine what sets your jewelry apart from competitors. Unique design, quality craftsmanship, or ethical practices can all be part of your differentiation strategy.

4. Consistency: Maintain a consistent brand image in all your communications, from your jewelry pieces to your online presence and customer interactions.

Creating a Logo and Visual Identity

Your logo and visual identity are the visual representations of your brand. Here's how to craft them effectively:

1. Logo Design: Create a distinctive logo that encapsulates your brand's values and style. The design should be simple, memorable, and versatile for use on various platforms.

2. Color Palette and Typography: Choose a color palette and typography that align with your brand identity. Consistency in these elements helps reinforce your brand recognition.

3. Visual Elements: Beyond the logo, consider other visual elements like patterns, graphics,

and imagery that complement your brand's visual identity.

4. Branding Guidelines: Develop a set of branding guidelines that outline how your brand elements should be used to maintain consistency across all materials and platforms.

Storytelling and Branding

Effective storytelling is a powerful tool for brand building. Here's how to weave a compelling brand story:

1. Origin Story: Share the story of your jewelry-making journey, what inspired you, and the challenges you've overcome. Personal anecdotes resonate with customers.

2. Craftsmanship Stories: Narrate the processes and techniques you use to create your jewelry. Highlight the artistry and attention to detail.

3. Customer Stories: Share testimonials and experiences from satisfied customers to showcase the impact and value of your jewelry.

4. Mission and Values: Communicate your brand's mission and values. If you have a commitment to ethical sourcing or sustainability, convey these principles in your storytelling.

Establishing a Brand Voice

Your brand voice is how you communicate with your audience, and it should be consistent with your brand identity. Consider these factors:

1. Tone: Define the tone of your brand voice, whether it's casual, professional, informative, or playful. This tone should resonate with your target audience.

2. Language: Choose the language that your audience is most comfortable with, whether it's formal, conversational, or a combination of both.

3. Messaging: Create messaging that aligns with your brand's values and speaks directly to your customers' needs and desires.

4. Consistency: Ensure that your brand voice is consistent across all your communication channels, including social media, website content, and customer support.

Building an Online Presence

In today's digital age, establishing an online presence is crucial. Here's how to do it effectively:

1. Website: Create a professional website that showcases your jewelry, brand story, and contact information. Optimize it for search engines (SEO) to increase your online visibility.

2. Social Media: Select the social media platforms that align with your target audience, and consistently post content that reflects your brand identity.

3. E-commerce: If you plan to sell online, set up an e-commerce platform for your jewelry. Ensure a smooth shopping experience and secure payment options.

4. Content Marketing: Produce valuable content related to jewelry, craftsmanship, and your brand story. Blogs, videos, and tutorials can help attract and engage your audience.

5. Email Marketing: Build an email list to keep your audience informed about new collections, promotions, and brand updates.

Building a strong brand is an ongoing process that requires a deep understanding of your jewelry business, target audience, and industry trends. By crafting a compelling brand identity, creating a memorable visual presence, telling engaging stories, maintaining a consistent brand voice, and building a robust online presence, you can establish a brand that resonates with customers and sets your jewelry business on a path to success.

Chapter 9

Selling Your Jewelry

Chapter 9: Selling Your Jewelry

Selling your jewelry is a vital aspect of your jewelry-making business. This chapter delves into various methods and strategies for effectively selling your creations, whether through online channels, craft fairs, consignment, or wholesale.

Choosing the Right Sales Channels

Selecting the right sales channels for your jewelry business is crucial. Consider these options:

Online Marketplaces: Platforms like Etsy, eBay, and Amazon provide access to a large customer base. List your jewelry on these marketplaces to reach a global audience.

Personal Website: Setting up your own e-commerce website offers control over your brand and customer experience. You can showcase your jewelry, tell your brand story, and sell directly to customers.

Social Media: Utilize social media platforms like Instagram, Facebook, and Pinterest to showcase your jewelry, engage with your audience, and promote your brand.

Brick-and-Mortar Store: If you have a physical storefront, you can sell your jewelry directly to customers. Your store should reflect your brand's identity and create a unique shopping experience.

Popup Shops: Consider participating in popup shops and temporary retail events to reach a local audience and test the market.

Setting Up an Online Store

If you opt to sell your jewelry online, here are key considerations:

E-commerce Platform: Choose a suitable e-commerce platform, such as Shopify, WooCommerce, or BigCommerce, and design an attractive and user-friendly online store.

Product Listings: Create appealing product listings with high-quality images, detailed descriptions, and pricing information.

Payment and Shipping: Set up secure payment gateways and establish shipping and return policies that provide a seamless shopping experience.

SEO and Marketing: Optimize your online store for search engines (SEO) and implement digital marketing strategies to attract visitors and convert them into customers.

Customer Support: Provide excellent customer support, including responsive communication, order tracking, and assistance with inquiries.

Selling at Craft Fairs and Markets

Craft fairs and markets are excellent opportunities to sell your jewelry in person. Here's how to make the most of these events:

Event Selection: Choose the right craft fairs and markets that align with your target audience and brand.

Booth Setup: Create an inviting and aesthetically pleasing booth with proper lighting and displays that showcase your jewelry effectively.

Inventory Management: Prepare sufficient inventory to meet the demands of the event. Consider offering exclusive pieces or promotions.

Payment Methods: Provide multiple payment options, including credit card processing, to accommodate various customer preferences.

Branding: Ensure your booth reflects your brand identity and communicates your brand story.

Consignment and Wholesale

Consider consignment and wholesale as additional sales channels:

Consignment: Collaborate with local boutiques or online stores to place your jewelry on consignment. You'll receive payment once the jewelry sells, but keep in mind the consignment terms.

Wholesale: Selling wholesale involves providing your jewelry to retailers at a discounted price. Ensure you have a clear wholesale pricing structure in place and offer incentives for larger orders.

Marketing and Promotion Strategies

Effective marketing and promotion are essential to drive sales:

Social Media Marketing: Utilize social media to showcase your jewelry, engage with customers, and run targeted advertising campaigns.

Email Marketing: Build an email list and send newsletters with updates, promotions, and information about your jewelry.

Content Marketing: Create valuable content such as blog posts, tutorials, and videos related to jewelry-making.

This not only attracts potential customers but also establishes you as an expert in your field.

Influencer Collaborations: Partner with influencers in the fashion or jewelry niche to reach their followers and gain exposure.

Online Advertising: Use online advertising channels like Google Ads and Facebook Ads to reach a broader audience.

Networking and Building Relationships

Building relationships with customers and industry contacts can lead to valuable opportunities:

Customer Relationships: Provide exceptional customer service to build lasting relationships with your customers. Encourage reviews and referrals.

Industry Networking: Attend jewelry trade shows, workshops, and events to connect with other jewelry makers, suppliers, and potential partners.

Collaborations: Collaborate with other businesses, such as fashion designers or accessory stores, to expand your reach.

Local Community: Get involved in your local community through charity events, art exhibitions, or partnerships with local businesses.

Selling your jewelry is a multifaceted process that requires careful consideration of the right sales channels, effective online store setup, successful participation in craft fairs and markets, consignment and wholesale strategies, and comprehensive marketing and promotion. Networking and building relationships further enhance your presence in the jewelry industry and contribute to your business's long-term success.

Chapter 10

Legal and Business Considerations

Chapter 10: Legal and Business Considerations

Running a jewelry business involves several legal and business aspects that are essential for its success and longevity. This chapter explores key considerations, including business registration, intellectual property protection, taxation, insurance, and business planning.

Registering Your Jewelry Business

Formalizing your business is a critical step to establish credibility and ensure compliance with legal requirements. Consider the following:

Business Structure: Choose the appropriate business structure, such as a sole proprietorship, LLC, partnership, or corporation, based on your needs and preferences.

Business Name: Register your business name, also known as a "Doing Business As" (DBA) or trade name, if it differs from your legal name.

Business Licenses: Obtain any required business licenses or permits at the local, state, or federal level.

EIN: If you plan to hire employees or have multiple owners, apply for an Employer Identification Number (EIN) with the IRS.

Copyrights and Trademarks

Protecting your jewelry designs and brand identity is crucial to prevent intellectual property theft. Here's what to consider:

Copyrights: Understand how copyrights protect your original designs, including drawings, photographs, and written descriptions.

Trademarks: Consider trademarking your business name, logo, or specific jewelry lines to establish brand recognition and prevent others from using similar marks.

Intellectual Property Records: Maintain detailed records of your design concepts, drafts, and dates of creation to establish ownership in case of disputes.

Taxes and Accounting

Compliance with tax laws and proper accounting practices are fundamental for the financial health of your business:

Tax Identification: Ensure you have the necessary tax identification numbers and are aware of tax obligations, including income, sales, and use taxes.

Accounting System: Implement an accounting system to keep track of your income, expenses, and financial records. Consider using accounting software or hiring an accountant.

Tax Deductions: Familiarize yourself with tax deductions and credits available to jewelry businesses, such as deductions for materials and studio space.

Quarterly Payments: If you're self-employed, be prepared to make quarterly estimated tax payments to cover your tax liabilities.

Insurance for Jewelry Makers

Jewelry makers should consider various types of insurance to protect their businesses:

Business Liability Insurance: Protects your business from claims of injury or property damage caused by your products or services.

Product Liability Insurance: Covers you in the event of a lawsuit related to product defects or injuries caused by your jewelry.

Property Insurance: Protects your business property, including equipment, inventory, and studio space, from damage or theft.

Professional Liability Insurance: Offers protection in case of errors or omissions in your work, particularly if you offer design or consulting services.

Business Plans and Strategies

Developing a well-thought-out business plan and strategies is essential for guiding your jewelry business to success:

Business Plan: Create a comprehensive business plan that outlines your business goals, target market, marketing strategies, and financial projections.

Marketing Strategies: Develop effective marketing and sales strategies, both online and offline, to reach your target audience and promote your jewelry.

Financial Planning: Establish a financial plan that includes budgeting, pricing strategies, and growth projections for your business.

Growth and Exit Strategies: Consider long-term growth and exit strategies, such as expansion, franchising, or selling your business.

Legal and business considerations are the foundation of a successful jewelry business. Registering your business, protecting your intellectual property, understanding tax and accounting obligations, securing the right insurance, and developing comprehensive business plans and strategies ensure that your business operates legally, financially sound, and prepared for growth and unforeseen challenges.

Chapter 11

Managing Your Jewelry Business

Chapter 11: Managing Your Jewelry Business

Managing your jewelry business effectively is crucial for its growth and sustainability. In this chapter, we'll explore various aspects of business management, from inventory and customer service to shipping, returns, and scaling your operations.

Inventory Management

Proper inventory management is essential to ensure that you have the right materials and finished jewelry pieces on hand:

Materials Inventory: Keep track of your raw materials, such as gemstones, metals, beads, and findings, to avoid running out of essential supplies.

Finished Jewelry: Maintain an organized system for tracking your finished pieces, including categorizing and labeling them for easy retrieval.

Inventory Software: Consider using inventory management software to streamline the tracking process and receive alerts for restocking materials.

Stock Control: Implement efficient stock control processes to minimize waste, reduce the risk of theft, and prevent overstocking or understocking.

Customer Service and Communication

Providing excellent customer service is essential for building a loyal customer base:

Prompt Communication: Respond to customer inquiries and requests in a timely manner, providing clear and helpful information.

Personalization: Build relationships with your customers by remembering their preferences, offering personalized recommendations, and addressing them by their name.

Transparency: Be transparent about your products, including materials used, pricing, and any customization options.

Feedback Collection: Encourage customer feedback and reviews to improve your products and services. Consider running surveys or offering incentives for feedback.

Problem Resolution: Resolve customer issues or complaints professionally and promptly, aiming for a satisfactory resolution.

Shipping and Packaging

Efficient shipping and attractive packaging enhance the customer experience:

Shipping Partners: Choose reliable shipping partners with options for tracking and insurance to ensure safe delivery.

Packaging Materials: Invest in high-quality packaging materials, including boxes, protective padding, and branded packaging for a professional presentation.

Shipping Costs: Clearly communicate shipping costs to customers and consider offering free or discounted shipping for certain order amounts.

Shipping Times: Specify expected shipping times and follow through to meet or exceed customer expectations.

Handling Returns and Repairs

Establish clear policies for handling returns and repairs to maintain customer trust:

Return Policy: Develop a return policy that outlines the conditions under which returns are accepted, the process for returns, and any associated costs.

Repairs: Provide repair services for your jewelry, specifying the types of repairs you can accommodate and associated costs or warranties.

Customer Education: Educate your customers about proper jewelry care and maintenance to reduce the frequency of returns and repairs.

Scaling Your Business

As your business grows, consider how to scale effectively:

Outsourcing: Assess tasks that can be outsourced, such as administrative work, to free up your time for creative and strategic tasks.

Hiring: If needed, hire additional staff or collaborators to assist with production, marketing, customer service, or other areas of your business.

Technology Integration: Invest in technology and systems that improve efficiency, such as order management software, accounting software, or customer relationship management (CRM) tools.

Expanding Product Lines: Consider diversifying your product offerings, such as adding new jewelry lines, custom services, or related products.

Market Research: Continuously conduct market research to identify new opportunities, target markets, or trends to guide your business expansion.

Effective management of your jewelry business involves organized inventory management, exceptional customer service, efficient shipping and packaging, clear policies for returns and repairs, and strategic planning for business growth and scalability. By excelling in these areas, you can build a thriving and sustainable jewelry business.

Chapter 12

Evolving as a Jewelry Maker

Chapter 12: Evolving as a Jewelry Maker

As a jewelry maker, your journey is marked by continuous growth and evolution. This chapter explores various aspects of personal and professional development, creativity, and adaptability in the dynamic world of jewelry making.

Continuing Education and Skill Development

To remain competitive and innovative in the jewelry industry, ongoing education and skill development are crucial:

Workshops and Courses: Attend workshops, courses, and seminars related to jewelry making, design, and new techniques. These can be in-person or online.

Mentorship: Seek mentorship or guidance from experienced jewelry makers who can provide insights, share their expertise, and offer constructive feedback.

Self-Study: Continuously research and learn on your own through books, articles, videos, and industry publications. Stay updated on new materials, tools, and technologies.

Skill Diversification: Explore various jewelry-making techniques and styles, such as metalsmithing, stone setting, enameling, or beading, to expand your skill set.

Staying Inspired and Creative

Maintaining your creative spark is essential to creating unique and compelling jewelry:

Nature and Travel: Draw inspiration from the natural world, travel experiences, and cultural influences. Incorporate elements from your surroundings into your designs.

Art and Design: Explore other art forms, such as painting, sculpture, or fashion, to find fresh ideas and design concepts.

Mood Boards: Create mood boards or design journals to collect and organize images, color palettes, and concepts that inspire your work.

Collaborations: Collaborate with other artists, designers, or even customers to infuse new perspectives into your jewelry.

Artistic Challenges: Participate in challenges or competitions within the jewelry-making community to push your creative boundaries.

Adapting to Trends

The jewelry industry is influenced by ever-changing trends, and staying current is essential for market relevance:

Market Research: Regularly conduct market research to identify emerging trends, customer preferences, and changing fashion movements.

Trend Incorporation: Adapt your designs to incorporate trending styles or materials while retaining your unique brand identity.

Limited Collections: Consider creating limited collections or seasonal pieces that align with popular trends.

Customization: Offer customization options so customers can personalize their jewelry according to current trends.

Expanding Your Product Line

Diversifying your product line can attract a broader audience and generate additional revenue streams:

New Collections: Introduce new collections that cater to different styles or themes, appealing to a wider customer base.

Custom Work: Offer custom design services for clients who seek one-of-a-kind pieces or personalized jewelry.

135

Related Products: Consider expanding into related products, such as jewelry accessories, home decor, or jewelry-making kits.

Collaborations: Collaborate with other artists or brands to create exclusive, co-branded products.

Balancing Passion and Business

Maintaining a healthy balance between your passion for jewelry making and the practicalities of running a business is crucial:

Time Management: Allocate time for both creative work and business tasks, such as marketing, accounting, and customer service.

Business Planning: Develop a clear business plan that aligns with your creative goals, ensuring that both aspects work together harmoniously.

Delegate and Outsource: Consider delegating or outsourcing tasks that are not within your expertise to free up time for creative pursuits.

Wellness and Self-Care: Prioritize your well-being by taking breaks, practicing self-care, and avoiding burnout, which can negatively impact your creativity.

Evolving as a jewelry maker involves a commitment to lifelong learning, staying inspired, adapting to trends, expanding your product line, and finding a harmonious balance between your creative passion and the demands of running a successful jewelry business. This ongoing process ensures that your journey as a jewelry maker remains fulfilling and dynamic.

Conclusion

Celebrating Your Journey in Jewelry Making and Selling

As you reach the conclusion of your jewelry-making and selling guide, it's a time for reflection, celebration, and looking forward to your bright future in the world of jewelry. Let's explore this concluding section in detail:

Celebrating Your Journey in Jewelry Making and Selling

Acknowledging Your Achievements: Take a moment to acknowledge and celebrate your journey so far. Whether you're just beginning or have been crafting and selling jewelry for some time, remember that every step you've taken has been an achievement.

Showcasing Your Creations: Celebrate by showcasing your creations. Share your jewelry pieces with friends, family, and customers. Consider hosting a jewelry show or exhibit to display your work and share your passion with the world.

Customer Appreciation: Celebrate your customers who have supported your jewelry-making venture. Consider running special promotions or offers as a token of your gratitude. Happy customers can become your most loyal advocates.

Encouragement and Final Tips

Embracing Continuous Learning: The world of jewelry is ever-evolving, so never stop learning. Stay open to new techniques, materials, and design trends. Consider taking advanced courses or attending workshops to expand your skills.

Networking and Community: Join jewelry-making communities and networks. Connecting with fellow artisans can provide inspiration, guidance, and a sense of belonging. Share your experiences and be open to collaboration opportunities.

Balancing Passion and Business: As you continue your journey, remember the delicate balance between your passion for jewelry making and the business side of things. Maintain your love for the craft while also running a successful venture.

Setting Goals: Set clear goals for your jewelry business. Whether it's about expanding your product line, reaching a certain number of customers, or achieving a specific revenue target, having goals keeps you motivated and focused.

Adapting to Trends: Stay attuned to changing consumer preferences and industry trends. Adapt your designs and marketing strategies to remain relevant and appealing to your target audience.

Eco-Friendly Practices: Consider adopting eco-friendly practices in your jewelry making. With growing awareness of sustainability, incorporating recycled materials or responsible sourcing can attract environmentally conscious customers.

Quality Over Quantity: Prioritize quality in your jewelry. Craft pieces that are not only beautiful but also durable. Quality jewelry builds trust and customer loyalty.

Remember the Joy: In the midst of managing a jewelry business, don't forget the joy that jewelry making brings you. Let your passion shine through in your creations and interactions with customers.

Self-Care: Running a jewelry business can be demanding. Take care of yourself physically and mentally. Regular breaks and self-care routines will ensure your long-term well-being.

Seek Inspiration: Seek inspiration from diverse sources, be it nature, art, culture, or history. Inspiration can lead to innovative designs that set you apart in the jewelry market.

In your jewelry-making and selling journey, remember that it's not just about the jewelry itself but the creative process, the connections you make, and the personal and professional growth you experience along the way. Each piece you create carries a piece of your story and your artistry, and that's something worth celebrating. So, embrace your journey, stay encouraged, and let your jewelry-making passion continue to shine in the years ahead.

About the Author

Sydney Brown has spent over thirty-five years in the business world and later in the corporate world. She has learned what works and what doesn't when the goal is to get out of the stale, vanilla world of the generations before us.
She believes that each person has at least one successful business, one book, and one grand adventure in them, but most people don't know how to figure out their best fit, so they stay where they are.

She is a best-selling author, speaker, and coach, helping people reach out of their current situation and reinvent themselves so they can do more than exist and survive while in this great space.
Personally, she's a mom of two adulting children and proudly owns the title of "Crazy Cat Lady" among her friends. After too many years of avoiding living life, she is on a mission to help others identify and begin their own "Great Ascension."

Let's Connect

If you've enjoyed this book, you'll love what else is ahead!
Start out at https://beyourownsolution.com/ and see what you can look forward to.
We have courses, certifications, and life and business focused free groups!

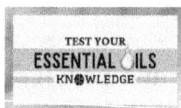

Free Essential Oil Quiz

Click to Sign Up

Aromatherapy Alchemy: Gateway to Wellness

Click to Sign Up

Project Flow Mastery: Universal Laws at Work

Click to Sign Up

Life in Flow: Path Toward Personal Wellness

The Inner Circle

Free Groups:
https://www.facebook.com/groups/fundsfriendsfutures
https://www.facebook.com/groups/shifttimes

Also From TLM Publishing House

FICTION –

Sydney Brown Presents Series

https://www.amazon.com/dp/B0BSBT36HN

The Mall Cadet Series

https://www.amazon.com/gp/product/B0B66MDK3T

All In or Nothing Series

https://www.amazon.com/dp/B0B7FW9W8M

The 7 Wishes Series

https://www.amazon.com/dp/B0B62XJY59

The Deception Series

https://www.amazon.com/dp/B0B5RNQMF1

The Forbidden Love Series (18+)

https://www.amazon.com/dp/B0B5SX24SX

The Essential Witch Chronicles

https://www.amazon.com/dp/B0CKSHS1H1

NONFICTION –

How to Start It Series

https://www.amazon.com/dp/B09Y2QHDPM

Aromatherapy Alchemy

https://www.amazon.com/dp/B0CJ5DD5C1

www.ingramcontent.com/pod-product-compliance
Lightning Source LLC
Chambersburg PA
CBHW061146040426
42445CB00013B/1570